Fife Council Education Department
King's Road Primary School
King's Crescent, Rosyth KY11 2RS

FOCUS ON EUROPE

BRITAIN
AND THE BRITISH

ANITA GANERI

FRANKLIN WATTS
LONDON • SYDNEY

This edition printed in 2001

Designed and produced by
Aladdin Books Ltd
28 Percy Street
London W1P 0LD

First published in
Great Britain in 1993 by
Watts Books
96 Leonard Street
London EC2A 4XD

ISBN 0-7496-3871-0

A CIP catalogue record for this book is
available from the British Library.

Printed in U.A.E.

Design	David West Children's Book Design
Designer	Flick
Series Director	Bibby Whittaker
Editors	Charles de Vere
	Sally Matthews
	Richard Green
Picture research	Emma Krikler
Illustrators	David Burroughs
	Peter Kesteven

The author, Anita Ganeri, has an M.A.
from Cambridge. She has written
numerous children's books.

INTRODUCTION

Britain is an island nation in north-western Europe. It consists of three countries; England, Scotland and Wales. For hundreds of years Britain has been one of the world's most important nations, in spite of its relatively small size. The British started the Industrial Revolution, founded the largest empire in history and have produced some of the world's greatest scientists, explorers, writers, artists and political leaders. This book offers an insight into Britain and the lives of the British people. It includes information about geography, language and literature, science and maths, history and the arts. The key below shows how these subjects are divided up.

Geography

The symbol of the planet Earth shows where geographical facts and activities are included. These sections include information on the great British explorers and the British Empire. Also discussed are Britain's sporting and commercial links with the rest of the world.

Language and literature

An open book is the sign for activities and information about language and literature. The historical origins of nursery rhymes and some of Britain's most famous writers are discussed here. The legends of Robin Hood and King Arthur are also included.

Science and maths

The microscope symbol indicates where information on science or maths is included. The making of Scotch whisky, the invention of television and the Industrial Revolution are explored in these sections.

History

The sign of the scroll and hourglass shows where historical information is given. These sections look at key figures and events in British history including the Norman Conquest and the English Civil War.

Social history

The symbol of the family indicates where information about social history is given. The Suffragette movement, different styles of houses in Britain, local festivals and traditional food are amongst the subjects covered in these sections.

Arts, crafts and music

The symbol showing a sheet of music and art tools signals arts, crafts or musical activities. This section explores the huge variety of music in Britain, from Elgar to the Beatles, the theatres of London and the architecture of Sir Christopher Wren.

CONTENTS

GREAT BRITAIN

Great Britain is made up of three countries – England, Scotland and Wales. Britain itself forms part of a larger group of countries called the United Kingdom of Great Britain and Northern Ireland, which is itself a full member of the European Union. It is separated from mainland Europe by the English Channel. It has a population of nearly 59 million, making it one of the world's most densely-populated countries. The Union Jack (above) is the flag of the United Kingdom.

English is the official language of Britain. It is derived from the Germanic languages spoken by the Anglo-Saxons and influenced by Norse, Latin and French. Today, English is the second most widely spoken language in the world after Chinese. It is the international language of business and is the second language spoken in many countries (see map, right).

The languages of Britain
Although English is spoken and understood throughout the whole of Britain, there are several regional languages which exist alongside it. About a fifth of

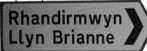

Welsh people speak Welsh, and children are encouraged to learn both Welsh and English at school. About a sixth of Scottish people, especially those living on the Hebrides, can speak their traditional language, Scots Gaelic. Both Welsh and Gaelic are Celtic languages, based on the languages spoken by the Celts who invaded Britain about 2,700 years ago.

■ English as mother tongue
■ English as second language

BBC World Service
The BBC World Service is a radio service which broadcasts worldwide to about 120 million people. Programmes are broadcast in English and in more than 35 other languages. There are news and current affairs programmes, sports, music and drama and an English-language teaching service.

Greenwich Mean Time

Time all over the world is worked out by how far a place is to the east or west of Greenwich, in south-east London. The line which marks 0° longitude passes through the old Royal Observatory at Greenwich. It is called the prime, or Greenwich, meridian. The time at Greenwich was originally shown by the 24-hour clock (right) and is known as Greenwich Mean Time (GMT). Today, time is measured by an atomic clock.

The Royal Family

The Royal Family attract tourists to Britain from all over the world. Buckingham Palace, the official London home of Queen Elizabeth II (below right) and Prince Philip, is open to the public between August and October. Members of the Royal Family make many public appearances and perform charity work. However, they are not as popular today with the British people as they once were.

England Patron saint – St George; feast day – 23 April; emblem – the red rose.

Scotland Patron saint – St Andrew; feast day – 30 November; emblem – the thistle.

Northern Ireland Patron saint – St Patrick; feast day – 17 March; emblem – the shamrock.

Wales Patron saint – St David; feast day – 1 March; emblems – the leek and the daffodil.

The Proms

Every summer, concerts of choral, orchestral and operatic music, both old and new, are held in the Royal Albert Hall (below). These Promenade Concerts, or "Proms", were founded by Sir Henry Wood in 1896 to bring classical music to the general public and they feature music and musicians from around the world. The Proms are extremely popular, particularly on the last night when the promenaders join in with songs such as *Rule Britannia*.

EARLY HISTORY

Little is known of the inhabitants of Britain before and during the Bronze Age, although Stonehenge (left) was completed at this time. The Celts arrived in the 8th century BC and with them came the Iron Age and the Celtic language. The Romans, led by Julius Caesar, followed in 55 BC and stayed until 410 AD. The country was then conquered by the Anglo-Saxons. In the 700s AD, the Vikings began to raid Britain and, in 1016, Canute was crowned king of England.

DATE CHART

c.2500 BC Stonehenge and Avebury stone circle are built.
2000-1000 BC The Bronze Age in Britain. People use bronze for tools, weapons and jewellery.
c.700s BC The Celts arrive, bringing with them the use of iron.
55 BC Julius Caesar invades.
43 AD The Roman Conquest begins, under Emperor Claudius.
c.122-128 AD Hadrian's Wall is built.
597 AD St Augustine brings Christianity to Britain from Rome.
793 AD The first Viking invasion.
878 AD King Alfred defeats the Danes and creates Danelaw giving the Danes certain areas in Britain to rule.
1016 AD Canute, the Danish king, becomes King of England.
1066 AD The Norman Conquest. William I defeats Harold II at the Battle of Hastings.
1086 AD The Domesday Book is compiled.
1154-1189 AD Henry II, the first Plantagenet king.
1199-1216 AD Reign of King John.
1215 AD King John signs the Magna Carta at Runnymede.
1337-1453 AD The Hundred Years War.
1348 AD The Black Death.
1455-1485 AD The Wars of the Roses.

The Bayeux Tapestry was embroidered in England in the late 1100s. It tells of the events which led up to the Norman Conquest and the death of King Harold in 1066. The tapestry is 70 metres long and 51 centimetres wide. It gives a valuable record not only of the history of the Conquest itself but of what people wore.

Hills and white horses

A huge horse like this one, originally dating from Saxon times, is carved into the chalk of Westbury Hill on the edge of Salisbury Plain in Wiltshire. It is so enormous that a group of people can stand comfortably in its eye. Another famous white horse is to be seen at Uffington in Oxfordshire. It is not clear when the 114 metre-long horse was first carved in the hillside, but it is now thought that it may be up to 2,000 years old.

King Arthur and Camelot
Legend has it that Arthur, son of Uther Pendragon, became King of England when he pulled a magical sword out of a stone. He reigned from Camelot, where he assembled the Knights of the Round Table. King Arthur was first mentioned in a Welsh poem dating from about 600 AD. Hundreds of stories have been written about Arthur, although historians are not entirely sure that he ever existed.

The Domesday Book
In 1085, William the Conqueror commissioned a survey of England. His officials recorded details of every village, together with exact numbers of people, cattle, pigs and goods owned, down to the last chicken. The result was the two-volume Domesday Book which is still used as a major historical source of information about Norman England. At the time, William used the survey to see how much tax he could charge.

The Hundred Years War between England and France began in 1337. King Edward III wanted to win back English lands in France. The English won the Battle of Crecy (left) in 1346 and the Battle of Poitiers in 1356. After a period of French recovery, the next great victory was at Agincourt in 1415, under King Henry V. Inspired by the leadership of Joan of Arc, the French fought back. When the war ended in 1453, England had lost all its French territories, apart from Calais.

In 1215, the barons and the Church forced King John (right) to sign a document called the Magna Carta, or "Great Charter". The document protected rights of the barons, the Church and the ordinary people and stopped the king interfering too much in what they did. The Magna Carta was signed at Runnymede in Surrey. Four copies of the document still exist.

The Church
Since Saxon times, Britain has been a mainly Christian country. The Saxons were converted by St Augustine, a Catholic missionary from Rome, and the Pope was accepted as the head of the Church. In Norman times, the Church remained an important influence on people's lives. Churches, cathedrals and monasteries were built all over the country. In the 16th century, however, King Henry VIII ended the Pope's authority and had himself proclaimed head of the Protestant Church of England. This period of Church history is called the Reformation.

Saxon

Norman

Early English

TUDORS TO THE PRESENT

The Wars of the Roses ended in 1485 in victory for the royal house of Lancaster over the royal house of York. The Lancastrian leader, Henry Tudor, was crowned King Henry VII. The Tudor age was a time of new ideas, world-wide exploration and prosperity, with strong rulers such as Henry VIII and Elizabeth I. The monarchy continued, apart from a short period in the 1650s, to the present day. In the 18th and 19th centuries, Britain expanded its power and territories overseas and built up a large empire. The 20th century, however, heralded the break-up of the British Empire.

The six wives of Henry VIII

Henry VIII came to the throne in 1509. His first wife was Catherine of Aragon. Henry desperately wanted a male heir and they only had a daughter, Mary. In 1527, Henry tried to divorce Catherine but the Pope refused him permission. Henry broke with Rome and made himself head of the Church. He then divorced Catherine and married Anne Boleyn. Anne had a daughter (Elizabeth I), but no son. Henry suspected her of adultery and had her beheaded. He then married Jane Seymour, who died giving birth to a son (Edward VI). Henry married three more times – to Anne of Cleves (divorced), Catherine Howard (beheaded) and Catherine Parr. Henry died in 1547.

Nursery rhymes

Many familiar English nursery rhymes have their origin in historical events. *Ring a ring o' roses* refers to the Black Death, or plague, which killed thousands of people in Britain in 1348 and 1665. *Mary, Mary, quite contrary* is thought to have been about Mary, Queen of Scots. *Little Boy Blue* was Cardinal Wolsey, one of Henry VIII's chief ministers and advisors. *Goosey, goosey gander* refers to the soldiers in Cromwell's army.

The Battle of Waterloo

The Battle of Waterloo was fought on 18 June 1815, near Brussels in Belgium. It marked the end of Napoleon Bonaparte's conquest of Europe. The British, led by the dashing Duke of Wellington and helped by Prussian, Austrian and Russian troops, succeeded in defeating Napoleon. He was exiled for a second time, on this occasion to the remote island of St Helena in the South Atlantic, where he died. The Duke of Wellington was greeted as a national hero. He was Prime Minister of Britain from 1828 to 1830.

English Civil War

The English Civil War (1642-1651) was fought between the Royalists (supporters of King Charles I), called "cavaliers" because of their wigs, and the Parliamentarians, led by Oliver Cromwell, and nicknamed "roundheads" because of their short haircuts. In 1649, Charles I was beheaded and Cromwell was put in charge of the newly-formed Commonwealth until his death in 1658. Then Charles I's son was crowned as Charles II.

Britain at war

World War I broke out in 1914, between the Allies (Britain, France, Russia and the USA) on one side and the Central Powers (Germany, Austria-Hungary and Turkey) on the other. The Allies were victorious but, by the time the war ended in 1918, some 10 million soldiers had been killed, 750,000 of them British. World War II (1939-1945) was fought between the Allies and the Axis powers – Italy, Japan and Germany, under the Nazi leadership of Adolf Hitler. Fighting took place in Europe, Russia, Africa, Asia and the Pacific. The death toll was horrific, with an estimated 50 million dead. Germany was defeated again, and the war against Japan ended with the dropping of the first atomic bomb on the Japanese city of Hiroshima on 6 August 1945.

REMEMBER BELGIUM

ENLIST TO·DAY

Churchill

Winston Churchill was one of Britain's greatest statesmen. He will always be remembered by the British as the man who gave them the will to fight on while towns and cities were being destroyed by German bombing raids during World War II. His forceful speeches also persuaded the Americans to lend Britain vital supplies and armaments, before the Americans themselves entered the war.

DATE CHART

1485 Henry VII is crowned King.
1509-1547 Reign of King Henry VIII.
1558 Elizabeth I becomes Queen.
1588 Spanish Armada defeated by the English.
1603 England and Scotland are united under the rule of one king, James I of England and James VI of Scotland.
1605 Guy Fawkes (right) leads the Gunpowder Plot to blow up the Houses of Parliament.
1642-1651 English Civil War.
1665 Outbreak of plague.
1666 The Fire of London.
1707 Act of Union. England and Scotland are united as the United Kingdom of Great Britain.
1775 Beginning of American War of Independence.
1800 Act of Union with Ireland.
1805 The Battle of Trafalgar.
1815 The Battle of Waterloo.
1837-1901 Reign of Queen Victoria.
1899-1902 Second Boer War.

Guy Fawkes

Plague doctor

1914-18 World War I.
1939-45 World War II.
1952 Elizabeth II becomes Queen.
1982 Falklands War.
1991 Gulf War.
1999 Balkans War.

INFLUENCE AND PRESENCE

For centuries, Britain has been one of the most influential countries in the world. Its scientists, explorers, inventors, engineers, writers and political leaders have been at the forefront of world affairs. Although forced to give up many of its territories after 1945, Britain still retains its members of the Commonwealth – an association of 54 independent states, 16 of which recognise the Queen as their Head of State, including Australia and New Zealand.

Exploration

The golden age of exploration began in the 15th century and lasted for more than 200 years. During the reign of Elizabeth I, many British sailors went in search of unknown lands. These included Sir Walter Raleigh, who led several expeditions to America, and Sir Francis Drake, who became the first Englishman to sail round the world between 1577 and 1580. Drake's successful battles against the Spanish helped England become a major sea power. He was knighted by Queen Elizabeth I for his courage, and for the treasures he brought back with him!

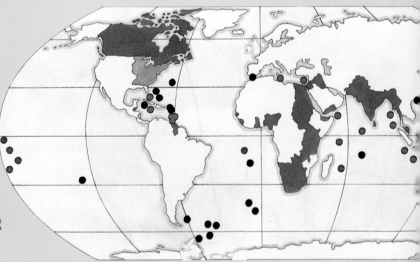

The British Empire – its rise ...

From the 17th to 19th centuries, Britain conquered and controlled a vast overseas empire. British influence spread all over the world, to North America, Australia, India and the West Indies. The main reason behind Britain's expansion was foreign trade. Cotton, sugar and tobacco were brought from the colonies to Britain for processing and sale. Political control of the colonies followed, the countries being ruled under British government and law.

The Suffragettes

The Suffragettes were members of a political and social organisation for women, founded in 1903 by Emmeline Pankhurst. Their aim was to campaign for more rights and recognition for women, including the right to vote in elections, and they campaigned vigorously. For many years, the government was reluctant to give women the vote and many Suffragettes were arrested and sent to prison. In 1918, women were given some voting rights. However, it took until 1928 for women to get full, equal voting rights with men.

A Suffragette seen here campaigning for equal voting rights.

The Great Exhibition of 1851 was devised by Prince Albert, Queen Victoria's husband, to display technical inventions from Britain and around the world. The exhibition was held in a brand new building of glass and iron, called the Crystal Palace. It was a great success and more than six million people attended.

George Stephenson's *Rocket*, built in 1829, was the fastest train of its age, travelling a speed of 48 kph.

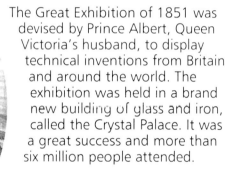

Industrial Revolution

In the late 18th and early 19th centuries, Britain changed from an agricultural to an industrialised society. A new process of smelting iron ore with coke saw the rapid expansion of the iron and coal industries. This period is called the Industrial Revolution. New steam-powered machines were invented and factories, cotton mills, potteries and ironworks grew up all over Britain. Many large towns and cities were established in these industrial centres. The effects of the Industrial Revolution were felt all over the world.

■ Britain's territories today
■ British territories in the 1920s
☐ Earlier British territories

... and fall

During the American War of Independence in the 18th century, Britain lost its American colonies. But it gained control of Australia and New Zealand instead. The British Empire reached the height of its power in the late 19th century, during the reign of Queen Victoria. For her, India was the "jewel in the crown". In 1931, Australia, Canada, The Irish Free State, New Zealand, Newfoundland and South Africa were granted independence. In the 1940s and 1950s, India and many other countries regained their independence. Some of these countries still belong to the Commonwealth.

THE COUNTRY

Although Britain is a fairly small island, it has a wide variety of landscapes. The countryside ranges from the windswept highlands of northern Scotland to the green valleys of Wales and the steep, chalk cliffs of southern England. Ben Nevis in Scotland is the highest mountain and The Fens in eastern England is the lowest-lying area of Britain. The Severn is Britain's longest river and Loch Lomond its largest lake. Britain has a temperate climate, with mild summers, cool winters and rain throughout the year.

Most of Wales is covered by the Cambrian Mountains (above). These are beautiful and dramatic. The south-west counties of England – Devon, Cornwall and Dorset – are very popular with holidaymakers. They enjoy warm summers and have a dramatic coastline, with huge cliffs like these in Dorset (below), deep bays and picturesque fishing villages.

The English lowlands have most of Britain's farmable land, industry and people. The lowlands are made up of broad plains, broken by low hills and ridges. Much of the land is a patchwork of fields and meadows.

Orkney Islands

Hebrides

SCOTLAND

Moray Firth

SCOTTISH HIGHLANDS

R. Spey

Ben Nevis ▲

Grampian Mountains

Atlantic Ocean

Loch Lomond

Firth of Forth

Edinburgh

R. Clyde

R. Tweed

SOUTHERN UPLANDS

Cheviot Hills

North Sea

NORTHERN IRELAND

Isle of Man

PENNINES

REPUBLIC OF IRELAND

Irish Sea

ENGLAND

R. Humber

R. Mersey

R. Trent

St. George's Channel

R. Dee

ENGLISH LOWLANDS

The Fens

R. Great Ouse

Cambrian Mts

R. Severn

R. Avon

WALES

Cotswolds

Chiltern Hills

London

R. Taff

Bristol Channel   Cardiff

R. Test

R. Thames

R. Exe

SOUTHWEST PENINSULA

English Channel

Channel Islands

FRANCE

The lowlands of Scotland (below) have Scotland's best farmland and most of its mineral resources.

Outlaws and monsters

Robin Hood was a legendary English hero who lived as an outlaw in Sherwood Forest, near Nottingham. He and his followers, called the Merry Men, stole from the rich and gave to the poor. Some scholars think that the character of Robin may have been based on a real outlaw, Robert Fitzrooth, Earl of Huntingdon, who lived in the 13th century. The Loch Ness Monster, or Nessie, is a large creature that many people believe lives in Loch Ness, in Scotland. The earliest known description of a strange creature in the loch dates from 565 AD, and since then thousands of sightings have been reported. The creature is supposedly up to 3 metres long with humps and a long, slender neck.

There are mountains in the north and west of Britain. The Scottish Highlands are wild and rugged. The Pennines are often called "the backbone of Britain" and stretch from Northern England to the Midlands. The Fens are a low-lying, flat plain, at or below sea level.

Traditional dress

The traditional dress of Scotland is the kilt, a knee-length, pleated skirt made from tartan. Tartan is usually woven from wool, in hundreds of different patterns and colours. Each Scottish clan (large family group) has its own tartan design like the one illustrated left. The British royal family tartan is called the Royal Stewart. Kilts are traditionally worn by men. To complete his costume, a Scotsman wears a sporran (pouch), a doublet (jacket), a bonnet (cap) and a plaid (length of material) pinned at the shoulder with a brooch. He may also carry a skene-dhu (small knife) tucked into his socks.

Art and landscapes

Britain has a long history of famous landscape painters who captured the life and beauty of the English countryside. Turner and Constable are two of the most famous, but there are many lesser known artists such as Berwick, who did many etchings like the one here, called *The Farmyard in Summer*.

TOWNS AND CITIES

About nine out of every 10 people in Britain live in towns and cities. Most of these are in England which has a greater population than Scotland or Wales. London is the capital and biggest city in England. Edinburgh is the capital city of Scotland. Cardiff is the capital of Wales. Many of Britain's towns and cities grew up and expanded during the Industrial Revolution, to house workers from the mines, mills and factories. Today, most British cities have a mixture of old and modern buildings.

Housing

About 80 per cent of British people live in houses, rather than flats, although there are large blocks of flats in most cities. Many people own their own homes. People who work in the cities may also live in suburbs on the outskirts of the city.

Multi-racial Britain

Since the 1950s, people from Britain's former colonies, such as India, Pakistan and the West Indies, have settled in Britain. They have faced many difficulties, such as racial prejudice. Yet their cultures, languages and religions have made Britain a much richer, multi-racial society. There are now Muslim mosques (shown left), Sikh gurdwaras and Hindu temples, alongside Christian churches and Jewish synagogues.

Glasgow
Edinburgh
Newcastle
Bradford
Hull
Liverpool
Leeds
Sheffield
Manchester
Nottingham
Birmingham
Leicester
Coventry
Cardiff
London
Bristol
Southampton
Plymouth

New towns

Since 1946, 32 "new towns" have been built in Britain. The aim of these towns was to attract people and industries away from established towns and cities which were becoming very crowded and polluted, and to spread them more about the country. The biggest new towns were built around the outskirts of London. Milton Keynes (right) was one of the last of these towns to be built, in the early 1970s. The borough of Milton Keynes now has a population of about 207,000 people.

Historic towns

The town of Salisbury, in the south of England, is home to one of Britain's most beautiful cathedrals. Its 123m high spire is the tallest in England. Salisbury Cathedral (below) is unique among medieval English cathedrals as it was planned and built in one lifetime rather than over several centuries. Its foundations were laid in 1220 and it took 60 years to complete.

In the 1st century AD, the Romans built bath houses around the hot mineral springs in the English town of Bath. The ruins of the Roman baths were rediscovered in the 1760s. Bath enjoyed a revival as a spa town in the 18th century, when people visited to bathe in its healing waters (right). Much of the present city was built at this time. Today, Bath is one of Britain's most popular tourist cities.

Arts in the regional cities

Music, theatre, art and museums are all a feature of Britain's cities. There are six principal orchestras outside London, including Hallé Orchestra of Manchester and the City of Birmingham Symphony Orchestra.

The Royal Shakespeare Company at Stratford-upon-Avon is world famous for its mainly Shakespearian programme, while touring theatre companies often show their plays in other parts of the country before performing in London.

Of the many provincial museums, the most unusual is in York in northern England. A thousand years ago, York, or Jorvik as it was called by the Vikings, was one of the most important towns in Britain. In 1976, the remains of the original Viking town were found. Everyday objects and parts of houses had been perfectly preserved in the peaty soil. A Viking street has now been reconstructed underground, complete with all the sights, sounds and even smells of Viking life.

Beside the seaside

Seaside resorts attract millions of British holidaymakers every year. On the south coast of England, Brighton's attractions include a long seaside pier (below) and an exotic Royal Pavilion. Other popular resorts include Blackpool in the north-west, Scarborough in the north-east, and the Welsh seaside towns, such as Barry Island.

The Mersey sound

Liverpool is a major industrial city and port on the River Mersey. In the 1960s, several local pop music groups became internationally successful. Beatlemania swept the world. The Beatles – John Lennon, Paul McCartney, George Harrison and Ringo Starr – all grew up in Liverpool.

LONDON

London is the capital of England and Britain's biggest city. It is Britain's cultural and financial centre and the seat of its government. Over seven million people live in and around London. Many more work in the city and millions of tourists visit every year. London grew up on the site of the Roman port of Londinium, on the banks of the River Thames. Its original centre is now known as the City and is London's financial and banking district.

London Transport

The quickest way to get around London is by underground, or "tube". This is the oldest underground railway in the world. Steam trains began running from Paddington to Farringdon Street on the Metropolitan Line in 1863. Today's trains run by electricity. London is also famous for its double-decker buses (right) and for its black taxis. Public transport is seen as one possible solution to London's city-centre congestion.

Theatreland

London theatres are famous all over the world, and many shows are sold out for months ahead during the tourist season. Performances include plays, old and new, and musicals, such as *Cats* and *Les Miserables*. Some plays travel around the country before being put on the West End. The Royal Shakespeare Company performs in the Barbican Centre in east London. Shakespeare's Globe Theatre, originally built in 1587, was excavated in the 1980s and has since been rebuilt in the original style. Plays have been performed there since 1997.

The Old Vic (above) and the Globe Theatre (right)

The Tower of London

The Tower of London was begun in 1079 by William the Conqueror as a fortress. The White Tower was built first. Later kings added huge walls and a moat around it. Over the centuries, the Tower has served as a royal palace, a zoo, a prison and place of execution and, today, as a museum where the Crown Jewels are displayed. Legend has it that if the ravens living in the Tower grounds ever fly away, the kingdom will fall.

Colourfully uniformed Beefeaters guard the Tower and the Crown Jewels.

Tower Bridge (below) lies at the edge of the City. To the west is the City of Westminster, with Buckingham Palace, Westminster Abbey, the Houses of Parliament and Big Ben (top left) among many famous landmarks. Buckingham Palace is the London residence of the British monarch and is at the end of the Mall. The red-coated troops of the Queen's Household Cavalry perform their famous Changing of the Guard ceremony each day in the front courtyard of the Palace. The West End of London is the heart of London and contains many of the best-known names – Piccadilly Circus with its statue of Eros, Trafalgar Square with Nelson's Column, Leicester Square, Regent Street, Oxford Street and Soho. Further west lies Harrods, London's most famous department store, close to the fashionable areas of Chelsea and Kensington.

Wren and St Paul's

In 1666, large parts of London were destroyed by fire. The architect Christopher Wren (1632-1723) redesigned some of the damaged buildings. He built St Paul's Cathedral, one of London's most famous landmarks. Inside its great dome is the Whispering Gallery. If you whisper into the wall on one side, you can be clearly heard 368 metres away on the other side.

Carnival!

The Notting Hill Carnival is the biggest street festival in Europe. It is held at the end of August, over the bank holiday weekend. The West Indian-based carnival was first held in 1966. It features elaborately decorated floats, dancers in brightly coloured costumes and music from steel bands. The carnival is getting more and more popular – in 2000 over two million people attended.

RURAL BRITAIN

The British countryside is dotted with small towns and villages. Some of these villages have a green, a church and thatched cottages. Others have developed around coal mining areas or fishing ports. Much of rural Britain is very picturesque. Only about a tenth of British people live in the countryside, and, in many places, traditional village life has almost entirely disappeared as young people have moved to the cities to find work. At the same time, many older people have retired to the peace and quiet of the countryside.

Public houses

Public houses, or pubs, are a focal point of British social life, both in the countryside and in the cities. For hundreds of years, they have been places where people could enjoy a drink and a chat with their friends. The traditional British pub drink is beer, made from hops. The oldest pub in Britain is The Fighting Cocks in St Albans. It dates from the 11th century.

Traditional festivals

In many parts of the countryside, local festivals and ancient traditions are still celebrated. Guy Fawkes Night on 5 November is celebrated all over Britain with bonfires and fireworks. In some villages, May Day (1 May) is a time for dancing round a ribbon-draped maypole. This is an ancient spring festival dating back to medieval times. Morris dancing dates back to early pagan man and is still popular today. The dances are complex and involve the use of ribbons, bells and sticks. They are based on ancient fertility rites.

Morris dancers (above) and a maypole (right)

National Trust

The National Trust for Places of Historic Interest or Natural Beauty owns or protects more than 248,000 hectares of land and 200 buildings and gardens in Britain, such as Ham House in Twickenham, London. The National Trust was founded in 1895 and is one of the oldest conservation bodies in the world. It seeks to preserve many famous houses and areas recognised for their special fauna and flora.

Gardening is one of the most popular leisure activities in Britain. Most homes have a garden of some sort. This may be a flower border, a herb garden or just a window box. There are also many beautiful landscaped gardens to visit, such as those at Sissinghurst Castle in Kent. The Royal Botanical Gardens, commonly known as Kew Gardens, in Richmond, London is an important botanical research centre. Members of the public can also visit the largest collection of living and preserved plants in the world.

House styles

Traditional country cottages come in a range of styles, depending on which part of Britain they are in and what building materials were available at the time.

Some cottages have thatched roofs, made of dried reeds. Thatched roofs were once commonplace in the English countryside, but they are now increasingly rare as they are extremely expensive. Half-timbered buildings were popular in Tudor times. They were constructed from wattle and daub – wood overlaid with plaster. Welsh cottages have been built of slate and stone from local quarries for hundreds of years.

Thatched cottage

Tudor

Historic places to visit

The ancient stone monuments at Avebury (c.2600 BC) and Stonehenge (c.2500 BC) date from the Bronze Age. Hadrian's wall was built in 122 AD by the Emperor Hadrian to keep Scottish tribes out of Roman Britain. The Royal Family occupies a number of residences outside London. These include Windsor Castle, Sandringham in Norfolk and Balmoral Castle in Scotland.

Welsh cottage

ORGANISATION

For many years, the British countries were ruled by one government based at Westminster in London. In the late 1990s, certain powers were devolved (transferred) to Wales and Scotland. Now there is a Welsh Assembly and a Scottish Parliament, as well as the Parliament at Westminster which still has responsibility for key legislation across the UK. General elections for Westminster have to be held at least every five years. All British citizens over the age of 18 have the right to vote as long as they are registered.

Queen Elizabeth II is head of state. She has an important role to play, representing Britain at home and abroad. But it is Parliament which passes laws and governs the country. The Queen does not have any real political power. She is, however, formally consulted by the Prime Minister on important matters and formally opens Parliament in November.

Trade Unions

The trade unions are organisations which protect the jobs of working people. About 7 million people belong to trade unions. There are over 70 unions in the trade unions' national body, the Trade Union Congress (TUC), which was founded in 1868. The biggest is Unison, with over 1 million members, followed by the Transport and General Workers' Union. The first trade unions were set up after the Industrial Revolution when the miners and textile workers organised themselves into groups.

Bank of England

The Bank of England was established in 1694. It now acts as the government's bank, managing Britain's money and gold reserves. It is the only bank in England and Wales that is allowed to issue banknotes. About 5 million notes are printed or destroyed every day. In Scotland, several banks can print money. Scottish notes have the same value as those issued by the Bank of England and are legal tender across Britain.

Parliament is the supreme lawmaking body of Britain. It consists of the House of Commons and the House of Lords which assemble at the Houses of Parliament (left). The House of Commons has 650 elected MPs, including the government and the opposition. The Cabinet consists of about 20 ministers, each of whom runs a government department staffed by civil servants. Apart from the Welsh Assembly and Scottish Parliament, Britain is also divided up into units of local government, called counties and districts. Local councils deal with matters such as health, housing, roads and education in their areas.

Law and order

"Every person has the right to a fair trial if accused of an offence, and a person is presumed innocent until proved guilty." This is the fundamental principle of British law as practised by the law courts such as the Old Bailey (right). The police force in London was founded in 1829 by Sir Robert Peel. These constables were nicknamed "Bobbies" after him. Scotland Yard is the headquarters of the Criminal Investigation Department (CID) of the London Metropolitan Police.

EDUCATION & LEISURE

Education is an important part of British life. There are hundreds of schools, colleges and universities, including some of the most famous in the world. British people also find plenty of time for sport and leisure. Sports like football, rugby, cricket, tennis and golf are played or watched by many people, and sailing and other watersports are very popular. Gardening, walking and rambling are common outdoor pursuits, and many British people enjoy an active social life – millions go regularly to the cinema, the theatre, nightclubs or to live music venues.

International Sport

Britain competes regularly in international sport. A strong supporter of the Olympic movement, in 1948 Britain staged the first Olympic Games after the war. Today, British athletes compete in individual and team events all over the world. In football, England, Scotland, Wales and Northern Ireland play as individual countries. England has twice hosted major football tournaments – the World Cup in 1966 and the 1996 European Championships (Euro 96).

Education

In Britain, children go to school from the ages of 5 to 16. They attend a primary school until they are 10 or 11 years old, then go on to a secondary school. The state provides free education for children, although some attend private schools, where their parents pay the fees, and an increasing number of children are being educated at home. Some pupils stay on at school until they are 18 and then go to higher education at colleges or universities. Oxford (right) and Cambridge are the two oldest and most famous universities in Britain.

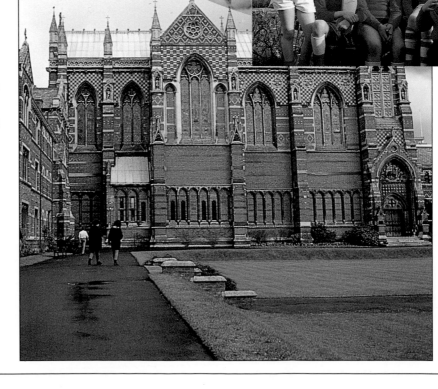

Festivals

Britain holds many musical and theatrical festivals throughout the year. These range from the Glastonbury Music and Arts festival in Somerset to the Glyndebourne opera festival in Sussex. Edinburgh Castle (built on an extinct volcano) hosts the Military Tattoo (left) during the Edinburgh Festival. There are also performances of opera, chamber and orchestral music and a "fringe" festival, where up-and-coming actors and comedians perform.

The National Youth Orchestra

Sport at home

Football (left) is the most popular team sport in Britain. Every Saturday, millions of fans attend matches to support their favourite clubs. Cricket is played all over England during the summer, with test matches held at Lords and the Oval in London and other grounds around the country. In June and July, the world's top tennis players compete in the Wimbledon championships.

British literature

British literature has a rich history. The oldest epic poem in English is *Beowulf*, probably composed in the 8th century. It tells of the hero Beowulf's battle against the monster, Grendel. Shakespeare is one of the most famous names in literature. He wrote 38 plays, including *Hamlet* and *Romeo and Juliet*. He also wrote many sonnets (a fourteen-line poem). Other famous poets include Burns, Wordsworth, Keats, Blake, Dylan Thomas and Shelley, husband of Mary Shelley who wrote the novel *Frankenstein*. Other great British novelists were Austen, Trollope, Defoe, Scott and Hardy. The Brontë sisters (pictured) grew up in Yorkshire in the mid-19th century. Their novels include *Jane Eyre* and *Wuthering Heights*. British literature has also provided many wonderful stories for children, including Lewis Carroll's *Alice's Adventures in Wonderland*. More recently, J K Rowling's *Harry Potter* series has proved popular with adults and children alike.

Invention of television

About 95 per cent of homes in Britain have a colour television set and watching TV is one of the most popular leisure pastimes. There are five main channels – BBC1, BBC2, ITV and Channels 4 and 5, in addition to the numerous channels that are now available from satellite and cable television. Although Britain generally has one of the highest standards in television, many programmes are imported, particularly from America. The first public demonstration of television was given by a Scottish engineer and inventor, John Logie Baird, in 1926. In 1936, the British Broadcasting Corporation (BBC) began to operate the world's first ever black and white television service.

AGRICULTURE AND FOOD

About three-quarters of the British countryside is farmland. About a third is used for growing crops and the rest is used for grazing sheep and cattle. The main crop-growing areas are in eastern and central southern parts of Britain. The major crops include wheat, barley, sugar beet and potatoes. Farming is now highly mechanised and efficient and only about 2 per cent of Britain's population work on farms. Farms produce about two-thirds of the food Britain needs. There are also rich fishing grounds around the coasts of Britain.

Britain's climate is very suitable for growing vegetables. Beet, potatoes, carrots, onions, peas, beans, cabbages and other green vegetables are produced in large quantities. The Berwick Street market in Soho, London (below) shows a typical selection of market produce.

Sheep

Fish

Oats

Beef cattle

Pigs

Poultry

Wheat

Sugar beet

Veg

Barley

Dairy

Fruit

Cattle and sheep are Britain's main types of livestock. Sheep are raised for their meat and their wool. The main areas for sheep farming are Wales, Yorkshire and Scotland. Cattle are raised for beef and milk production.

Great fields of yellow oilseed rape flowers are changing the face of the British countryside. Rape is grown for its oil and as cattle feed. Recently, production has risen to about 1.5 million tonnes a year.

Scotch whisky

The Scots have been making whisky since the 1400s. They now export more than 200 million litres of Scotch yearly, about half of which goes to the United States. Whisky is a strong, alcoholic drink made from grains such as barley, maize, rye and wheat. Scotch whisky is made mostly from barley. It is made by a process called distilling. Distillers first grind the grain and cook it in water, forming a mash. Later, malt and then yeast are added and the mixture is left to ferment. After fermentation the whisky is put in oak barrels for 2 to 12 years to age and develop its flavour and amber colour.

Cheese, hops and wool

Dairy farming provides milk for the hundreds of different types of cheeses made in Britain. Many cheeses take the name of the place where they are produced, for example, Cheshire, Gloucester and Caerphilly. Cheddar is probably the most popular cheese, while Stilton is considered the "King of Cheeses". Beer made from the hops of Worcestershire and Kent has a unique bitter taste, and there is a huge variety of beers brewed in regions around the country. Sheep farming provides wool for some of Britain's best-known products, such as Harris tweeds and Shetland knitwear.

Traditional grub

Many traditional British recipes originated hundreds of years ago. Pork pies were eaten in the 11th century, and the Elizabethans invented syllabub. Haggis (left) is the national dish of Scotland. It is made of sheep's liver, oatmeal and suet stuffed inside a sheep's stomach. It is eaten on special occasions such as Burns Night on 25 January, the birthday of the Scottish poet, Robert Burns.

Place names feature in traditional cooking, for instance, Yorkshire pudding (right), Lancashire hot pot and Cornish pasties. The 17th century habit of eating "high tea" is still popular in the north and west of Britain, and features many regional dishes, such as Welsh rarebit. Have a go at making your own Welsh rarebit. Melt 25 grams of butter in a saucepan, add 225 grams of sliced or grated Cheddar cheese, 1/4 teaspoon of English mustard, 3 tablespoons of milk, a dash of Worcestershire sauce, and salt and pepper. Stir until the cheese has melted and the sauce thickened, then serve on hot toast.

Fishing is a very important industry in Britain. About a million tonnes of fish are caught each year from the waters around Britain, and especially from the North Sea. The main types of fish caught are cod, haddock, plaice and mackerel.

INDUSTRY AND EXPORT

Britain is one of the world's leading industrial and trading nations. Its major exports are heavy machinery, aerospace equipment, oil and chemicals. Its major trading partners are Germany, the USA and France. Britain also has important service industries, such as tourism, banking and insurance. Britain has an extensive rail and road network, one of the largest merchant navies in the world and the world's busiest international airport, Heathrow.

Natural resources

For over 300 years, coal was heavily mined in Yorkshire, south Wales and Scotland. Today, however, many pits are being closed. Britain has large resources of iron ore but it is of low quality. Oil and natural gas were discovered in the North Sea in 1969 and Britain is a leading oil producer. The North Sea wells produce enough oil for Britain's domestic needs and for export. Britain is also a leader in nuclear technology. According to recent figures, the nuclear power industry now provides just under 30 per cent of Britain's electrical supply.

The products and expertise of many British companies are recognised throughout the world. The famous names include British Aerospace, which makes aircraft and military weapons; Rolls-Royce, the world's most luxurious cars; British Petroleum (BP) and Shell, the oil giants. Some famous companies, however, such as Rover Cars, have been bought up by foreign competitors.

ROVER

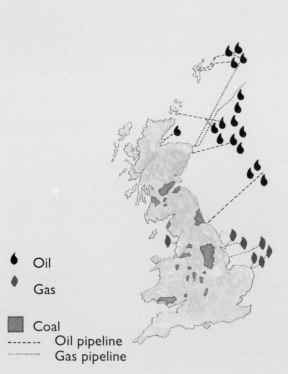

The music industry

British pop music is one of the country's most important and prosperous industries. British performers, such as the Beatles, David Bowie, Oasis and Spice Girls, have made names for themselves all over the world. Britain is known for music trends such as Punk, which burst onto the scene in the late 70s. One of the industry's greatest successes has been Virgin Records, founded by the entrepreneur Richard Branson. The Virgin Megastore (right) in London attracts thousands of record buyers every week.

◆ Oil

◆ Gas

■ Coal

------- Oil pipeline

.... Gas pipeline

Industries in decline

Shipbuilding, steel production and coal mining are some of Britain's traditional industries that have declined over recent years. Other manufacturers, particularly of cars, motorbikes like Triumph (right), electrical goods and computers, have suffered at the hands of Japanese and other Far Eastern competition. In the 1990s, Rover Cars was acquired by the German company BMW. Recently, however, Britain has attracted much overseas investment in manufacturing, particularly from Japan.

Some of Britain's largest companies are multinationals in the pharmaceutical industry. These include GlaxoSmithKline and ICI.

Military exports

British Aerospace, Rolls-Royce Aeroengines, Vickers, GEC, Westland and GKN are just some of the leading companies that have developed and marketed military weapons all over the world. The British Aerospace Hawk (below) has attracted substantial export orders.

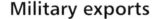

Wedgewood pottery

The pottery and porcelain in Britain is centred on an area around Stoke-on-Trent, called the Potteries. One of the best-known makes of British pottery is Wedgewood. Josiah Wedgewood (1730-1795) opened his first factory in the Potteries in 1759. Wedgewood pottery is made of blue or green stoneware, decorated with white, cameo-like patterns.

TODAY AND TOMORROW

Most of Britain's former colonies are now independent, and Hong Kong (left) reverted to China in 1997. In 1973, Britain became a member of the European Community, which has since evolved into the European Union (EU). Its armed forces (who are volunteers) play key roles in NATO and the United Nations. In addition, Britain has a special relationship with the United States, which involves close co-operation on world matters. Britain also maintains a nuclear submarine force.

The Channel Tunnel
The first proposal for a tunnel to be built under the sea between England and France was made by Napoleon in 1802. The idea was for people to travel in horse-drawn vehicles. Today, Eurostar trains operate between London Waterloo (below) and Paris and Brussels. They travel under the channel between England and France through over 30 kilometres of tunnel. The first journey was completed in 1994, and within five years over 10 million passengers had travelled by Eurostar.

Flag of the European Union

The European Union
Under the Treaty of Maastricht, EU member countries have agreed to new levels of co-operation on money and social matters.

Britain and the UN
As a member of the UN (United Nations), Britain has sent troops to Bosnia and Kosovo.

Flag of United Nations

Tourist trail
Tourism is one of Britain's most important industries, and it is growing. Over 25 million tourists visit Britain every year and 1.5 million people are employed to look after them. About 60 per cent come from Europe and about 20 per cent from the USA. The main tourist attractions are in London. People flock to see Buckingham Palace, the Houses of Parliament and Big Ben. Some come as students to learn English at summer schools, while others come to see the countryside, play golf or attend music festivals.

Britain has a long history of involvement in Ireland. Most people in Northern Ireland are Protestant and most in the south (Eire) are Catholic. The two groups have long been opposed in politics, with Protestants remaining loyal to British rule and Catholics wanting a united, independent Ireland. In 1969, the British government sent troops into Belfast after months of clashes between the two sides. After years of violence and thousands of murders, some progress has been made recently to give more independence to Northern Ireland. The future, however, remains uncertain.

Bomb damage in London as a result of "the Troubles" in Ireland.

It is hoped that the 1998 Good Friday Agreement will eventually lead to an end to British troops (left) in Northern Ireland.

ESA
The European Space Agency controls the space programme in Europe.

The London Stock Exchange (above) is one of the world's largest markets for stocks and shares in companies.

NATO
Britain was a founder member of the North Atlantic Treaty Organisation.

Charity work
Many British-based charities are working to help people in famine-stricken regions or in countries devastated by war, such as those in Africa and the former Yugoslavia. The Oxford Committee for Famine Relief, better known as OXFAM, was set up in 1942. It organises food aid and disaster relief. There is also a very active British branch of the Red Cross. Other fund-raising events include Comic Relief, a 24-hour television programme held once a year, which encourages people to donate money to different charities.

British inventors
Some of the world's most famous scientists, engineers and inventors have come from Britain. Michael Faraday (1791-1867) invented the electric motor. Alexander Graham Bell (1847-1922) invented the telephone. More recently, Sir Christopher Cockerell (born 1910) invented the hovercraft.

Britain has changed greatly during the 20th century and is continuing to change. It is adjusting to the challenge of its position as a multi-cultural society and to its role in Europe. At the same time, Britain is proud of its long history and keeps many traditions alive to this day.

FACTS AND FIGURES*

Name: Great Britain

Capital and largest city: London (population 7.7 million)

National anthem: *God Save the Queen*

Official language: English

Currency: Pound Sterling

Population: 58,744,000

Population density: 242 persons per km²

Distribution: 89% live in urban areas, 11% in rural areas.

Ethnic groups: White 94%, Asian Indian 2%, Pakistani 1%, Black Caribbean 1%, Black African 0.5%, other 1.5%.

Religion: Protestant (Anglican, Presbyterian, Methodist) 53%, Roman Catholic 10%, other Christian 3%, Muslim 2.5%, Hindu 0.5%, Sikh 0.5%, Jewish 0.5%, other (including nonreligious) 30%.

Climate: Temperate climate with mild summers, cool winters and moderate rainfall throughout the year.

Location: An island in Western Europe. France lies across the English Channel to the south; Ireland (Northern and Eire) to the west across the Irish Sea; and Belgium, the Netherlands, Germany, Denmark and Norway to the east across the North Sea.

Area: 242,900km²

Celsius
Above 5
4-5
3-4
Below 3

AVERAGE JANUARY TEMPERATURES

Celsius
Above 16
15-16
13-15
Below 13

AVERAGE JULY TEMPERATURES

Centimetres
More than 150
100-150
75-100
60-75
Less than 60

AVERAGE ANNUAL RAINFALL

Mountains: The Cambrian Mountains (Wales), the Grampian Mountains (Scotland) and the Pennines (England)

Highest mountain: Ben Nevis in Scotland, 1,343m

Longest river: the Severn in England, 354km

Largest lake: Loch Lomond in Scotland, 245km²

Physical features: Much of Britain consists of flat or rolling lowland, with rugged areas in Northern Scotland, Wales, the Pennines of northern England, and in Devon and Cornwall on the south-western peninsula of England. The Fens in eastern England lie at or below sea level.

Coastlines: On the North Sea, Irish Sea, North Altantic Ocean and English Channel.

AGRICULTURE

Crop production
Cereals, oilseed, potatoes and other vegetables.

Food/livestock production
Beef (cattle), lamb (sheep), pork (pigs), poultry and fish.

Land use
Pasture 45%, agriculture 25%, forests 10%, other 20%.

INDUSTRY
Production machinery, including machine tools, electric power equipment, automation equipment, rail and road equipment, shipbuilding, aircraft, motor vechicles and parts, electronics and communications equipment, metals, coal, petroleum, paper and paper products, food processing, textiles, clothing and other consumer goods.
A significant source of national income comes from the annual visit of 25 million tourists.

Imports
Machinery and transport equipment 42%, chemicals 10%, food 8%, clothing and footwear 4%, petroleum 3%, textiles 3%, paper 3%.

Major import sources:
Germany 15%, USA 12%, France 10%, Netherlands 7%, Japan 5%, Italy 5%, Belgium/Luxembourg 5%, Ireland 4%, Switzerland 3%, Spain 3%.

Exports
Machinery and transport equipment 44%, chemicals 13%, road vehicles 8%, petroleum 6%, food 4%, professional and scientific 4%, iron and steel products 2%.

Major export destinations:
Germany 12%, USA 12%, France 10%, Netherlands 8%, Ireland 5%, Belgium/ Luxembourg 5%, Italy 5%, Spain 4%, Sweden 3%, Japan 2%, Switzerland 2%.

ELECTRICITY
Production by source:
Thermoelectric	69.5%
Nuclear	27.5%
Hydroelectric	1%
Geothermal and other	2%

ECONOMY

The GDP (gross domestic product) is the amount of goods and services produced within a country. By dividing the GDP by the population a *per capita* result is reached.

Figures shown are the GDP per capita in the year 1997. (GDPs are shown in US dollars).

UK	21,927
USA	28,789
Germany	25,468
Belgium	23,948
Netherlands	23,270
Italy	19,962
Spain	13,412

*All figures given are for the UK as a whole.

Tourism is one of Britain's major industries.

FAMOUS FACES

LITERATURE

Geoffrey Chaucer
(c.1340-1400, right). The most influential poet of the Middle Ages; author of *The Canterbury Tales*.

William Shakespeare
(1564-1616, left). The greatest English playwright, author of lyric plays such as *A Midsummer Night's Dream*, historical plays like *Richard III* and famous tragedies including *Romeo and Juliet*, *Hamlet* and *Macbeth*.

Jane Austen (1775-1817). Novelist noted for her domestic novels of manners in middle class provincial society, such as *Pride and Prejudice*.

Charles Dickens (1812-1870, right). Novelist popular for his memorable characters and portrayals of the social evils of Victorian England. His novels include *Oliver Twist* and *Great Expectations*.

D H Lawrence
(1855-1930, left). English novelist and poet. His famous works include *Sons and Lovers*, *Women in Love* and *Lady Chatterley's Lover*.

George Orwell (1903-1950, right). Born Eric Arthur Blair, his best known novels are the political satire *Animal Farm* and *1984* with its fearsome portrayal of state control.

Graham Greene (1904-1992). Many of his works concern religious issues, and include *Brighton Rock*, *Our Man in Havana* and *Monsignor Quixote*.

ARTS

William Hogarth (1697-1764). British painter and engraver whose work, such as the series *A Rake's Progress*, made satirical comment on the morals of his time.

William Blake (1757-1827) was a poet, engraver and painter who invented his own mythologies to express his ideas.

J M W Turner (1775-1851, left). English landscape painter whose romantic works, such as *Rain, Steam and Speed*, were often flooded with brilliant, hazy light.

John Constable (1776-1837). Painted landscapes and coastal scenes all over Britain. *The Hay Wain* and many other paintings featured his native Suffolk.

Dante Gabriel Rossetti (1828-1882), poet and painter, was one of the founders of the Pre-Raphaelite Brotherhood. His paintings are noted for their rich colours.

William Morris (1834-1896). Influenced by the Pre-Raphaelites. Designer of textiles and wallpapers with beautiful, flowery patterns.

L S Lowry (1887-1976, above). He painted northern industrial townscapes and town life with characteristic matchstick figures.

Henry Moore (1898-1986). English sculptor known for his massive stone human-like forms.

David Hockney (1937- , right). British painter and designer and leader of the English Pop Art movement of the 1960s.

MUSIC

Henry Purcell (1659-1695, below left). His work marks the high point of Baroque music in England, and can be highly expressive. He wrote more than 500 works, which include the opera *Dido and Aeneas*.

W S Gilbert (1836-1911) **and A Sullivan** (1842-1900) wrote humorous operettas satirising Victorian society. Works include *The Mikado* and *H.M.S. Pinafore*.

Edward Elgar (1857-1934, below). Composed the *Enigma Variations* and the *Pomp and Circumstance* marches.

Frederick Delius (1862-1934). He wrote a whole range of music including choral works, operas, orchestral works, chamber music and songs.

Ralph Vaughan Williams (1872-1958). Best known for his choral-orchestral works; also wrote several symphonies.

Benjamin Britten (1913-1976, below). He wrote for the individual voice, for example Janet Baker, and is also known for his operas, including *Peter Grimes* and *The Rape of Lucretia*.

David Bowie (1947-). Highly influential pop singer and songwriter whose work spans five decades. His famous songs include *Space Oddity*, *Changes*, *Starman* and *Ashes to Ashes*.

Andrew Lloyd Webber (1948-). His musicals include *Jesus Christ Superstar*, *Cats* and *Phantom of the Opera*.

SCIENCE

Isaac Newton (1642-1727, right). Mathematician, astronomer and physician. Developed calculus and theories on gravity and motion.

James Watts (1736-1819). Inventor of the steam engine.

Charles Darwin (1809-1882). Scientist who developed the modern theory of evolution and proposed the principle of natural selection.

Alexander Graham Bell (1847-1922, left). Invented the telephone in 1876.

Alexander Fleming (1881-1955, right). Scottish bacteriologist who discovered the antibiotic drug penicillin. He got the Nobel Prize for Physiology and Medicine in 1945.

HISTORICAL FIGURES

Oliver Cromwell (1599-1658, left). Puritan leader of the Parliamentary side in the Civil War and, as Lord Protector, ruler of Britain from 1653 until his death five years later.

William Wilberforce (1759-1833). British reformer whose bill for the abolition of the slave trade led, in 1833, to the abolition of slavery throughout the British Empire.

Horatio Nelson (1758-1805, right). British admiral who led fleets against Napoleon in the Napoleonic wars. He won the Battle of Trafalgar in 1805.

William Gladstone (1809-1898). Political leader who came to power during the reign of Queen Victoria.

Winston Churchill (1874-1965, left). British politician who led a coalition government during World War II from 1940 to 1945. Also won the Nobel Prize for Literature in 1953.

Margaret Thatcher (1925- , right). Britain's first woman prime minister from 1979 to 1991.

KINGS AND QUEENS OF ENGLAND AND GREAT BRITAIN (Normans to present)

William I (1066-1087)
William II (1087-1100)
Henry I (1100-1135)
Stephen (1135-1154)
Henry II (1154-1189), left
Richard I (1189-1199)
John (1199-1216)
Henry III (1216-1272)
Edward I (1272-1307)
Edward II (1307-1327)
Edward III (1327-1377)
Richard II (1377-1399)
Henry IV (1399-1413)
Henry V (1413-1422)
Henry VI (1422-1461)
Edward IV (1461-1483)
Edward V (1483)
Richard III (1483-1485), above right
Henry VII (1485-1509)
Henry VIII (1509-1547)
Edward VI (1547-1553)
Mary I (1553-1558)
Elizabeth I (1558-1603), left
James I (VI of Scotland) (1603-1625)
Charles I (1625-1649), right
Commonwealth Council of State (1649-1653)
Oliver Cromwell - Protector (1653-1658)
Richard Cromwell - Protector (1658-1659)
Charles II (1660-1685)
James II (1685-1688)
William III (1689-1702) & Mary II (1689-1694)
Anne (1702-1714)
George I (1714-1727)
George II (1727-1760)
George III (1760-1820)
George IV (1820-1830)
William IV (1830-1837)
Victoria (1837-1901), above left
Edward VII (1901-1910)
George V (1910-1936)
Edward VIII (1936, 325 days)
George VI (1936-1952)
Elizabeth II (1952-), right

INDEX

Photographic Credits:
Abbreviations: t – top, m – middle, l – left, b – bottom, r – right
Cover, b, tr, back cover, 1, 4m, 4br, 5t, 6t, 6b, 10t, 11b, 12t, 13t, 13bl, 15tl, 16mr, 18t, 18m, 20m, 21b, 22t, 23b, 27t, 28br and inset, 29tr, 29b – Select Pictures. Cover ml, 27br – Wedgewood. Cover tl, 2t, 3, 4t, 4bl, 9r, 12m, 12b, 14t, 15tr, 15m, 16t, 16ml, 17t, 17m, 19 both, 20b, 20-21, 21tl, 21tr, 22 inset, 23t inset, 23tr, 24t, 24m, 25 all, 26t, 28ml, 28bl – Roger Vlitos. 2m, 9l, 10m – Mary Evans Picture Library. 2b, 6m, 11t, 13br, 15b, 23m – Hulton Deutsch. 5m – Bryn Cotton/Assignment Photographers/CORBIS. 17b, 22b, 23tl, 24br, 28mr, 29tm, 29m – Frank Spooner Pictures. 14m, 14b – Paul Nightingale. 18b – Keith Newell. 21m, 28t – Eye Ubiquitous. 22m – Christian Liewig; Temp Sport/CORBIS. 24bl – Richard Jackson. 26mr – Rover Cars. 27ml – ICI Paints. 26m – Brian Hunter Smart. 27mr – British Aerospace. 29tl – Spectrum Colour Library.